# Creative Basics

## 30 Days to Awesome Social Media Art

By

*Crystal Stine*

crystalstine.me
@crystalstine
#creativebasics

# What People Are Saying

## About Crystal

Crystal is smart, she knows what she's talking about, and I wish I knew everything she knows.

**Myquillyn Smith,** "The Nester"
Author of "The Nesting Place"

Crystal is full of faith, generous and innovative. She's not afraid to try new things, to take risks and go big. She is more than willing to share her wealth of knowledge and contagious joy with you. I have learned so much from Crystal as a virtual assistant and as a leader in social media.

**Aubrey Barela**
Virtual Assistant

## About "Creative Basics"

I've struggled for a long time with the technical aspects of blogging and especially graphics for my photos. As a food blogger, I have a good handle on iPhone photography but for the life of me, couldn't figure out how to make my graphics pop.

**With Crystal Stine's Creative Basics course, it's like she's sitting with you at your computer taking you step by step and helping you create beautiful graphics.**

In this course, you'll learn how to master both Pic Monkey and Canva and some iPhone apps as well. Crystal's course has helped me tremendously, and if you want to take your images to the next level, I encourage you to get this book!

Kate Battistelli

What a fun and helpful course! Crystal takes the reader step by step through the process of creating fun graphics, and she makes it incredibly user-friendly. The steps are not overwhelming and can be done in a day. She gives photos, resources, and examples of everything she teaches. I also love how encouraging she is along the way; it's like she's celebrating with us in our progress of learning to create graphics! I'm so thankful Crystal is willing to share her expertise in this area with others.

**Eryn Hall**
Host of the Declare Conference
MamaHall

# Preface

You open Instagram and see beautifully created graphics featuring inspirational quotes. Then you head over to Pinterest and wonder how you could make images like the ones you see. And after you sign up for a blogger's email list, you wish you could create a free printable for your site, to encourage your readers to sign up for YOUR list.

Over the next 30 days, you'll learn how to do all of that – and more.

I'm excited that you've decided to join me for this 30 day "Creative Basics" course. I'll take you from start to finish, creating everything from text-only graphics to quote images and quite a few things in between.

**What You'll Learn:**

- Where to find photos
- Some rules about fonts
- How to use Canva, PicMonkey, and a few of my favorite apps
- ...and by the end of it, you'll even create a free printable to offer your readers!

This is content that I typically share at conferences collected from over ten years of marketing, blogging and social media experience, all in one all-encompassing resource for you to work through at your preferred pace!

**What You'll Need to Get Started:**

- A computer (the majority of these sites work best when used on a computer, not a tablet or smartphone)
- A basic understanding of how to save and retrieve files to/from your computer
- Internet access
- A smartphone is optional, but several courses will involve using apps
- Social media accounts (Instagram, Facebook, Twitter, and Pinterest) are also optional, but the majority of this

content will focus on creating micro-content for those platforms

**Here's how it will work:**

Each day you'll find one challenge to tackle. Every course will build upon the one before so that, by the end, you'll have all the tools you need to create our final project – a free printable!

Easy, right? I promise we'll take it slow and work together. I'll share some examples, and you can check out the #creativebasics hashtag on Instagram to see what others are doing as well!

# Table of Contents

# Day 1 – "Mise en Place"

Grab your coffee and let's get started. I'll let you know right now that you're going to want to be patient with me through the first six days as we prepare to make some awesome images.

In cooking, what we're going to be doing on days 1-6 is called "mise en place," or if you aren't up on your French (coming from the gal who took Spanish & Italian) "putting in place." It's the essential organizing, arranging, and prep work that helps us make sure we have everything in order before we dive in!

But don't worry - this isn't a bait & switch course where I give you the bare minimum and then charge you a fee for the rest. I promise you'll leave having created more than 15 different types of images and learning every tip & trick I can think to share with you!

**Today's Challenge:**

Find at least one beautiful scenic photo to save to your desktop from Unsplash.

**The How-To:**

1. Go to Unsplash.com

2. Scroll through the images until you find one you like

3. Click on it to open it in a new window

4. Right-click to save the image to your desktop as a JPG

5. Repeat as needed

Unsplash is a great site that offers professional photographs that are completely free for you to modify as you wish. For zero dollars. When you're first starting to use photos from around the internet for your projects, understanding licenses and royalty-free options can be a challenge, so this is a great place to start!

Generally speaking, most photo sites ask that you do not use the image on anything you intend to make a profit on, and most will give suggested language on how to properly credit the photographer if they require it. While I might suggest sites during this course that I love to use, it's up to you to learn the terms of use and understand them before you do anything with the images!

We'll be building a little library over the next few days so that when we're ready to jump into creating graphics, we won't have to spend time hunting for a photo! On Day #3 I'll also share with you my pros & cons when it comes to using free images.

# Day 2 – Finding Photos

Were you able to find a scenic image on Unsplash yesterday? Or, if you're like me, maybe you ended up spending way too long looking at ALL the beautiful photos! Those are some incredibly talented photographers!

**Bonus Tip**: In case you found several images you'd love to use for future projects, you might want to create a folder on your desktop, Google Drive, or Dropbox called "Unused Images." You can save the images you find to one location (so you don't have to scroll forever trying to find it again), and when you've created blog graphics or social media images with it, you can move it to a new file called "Used Images." Just another little "mise en place" tool to help keep you organized!

**Today's Challenge:**

Head over to Pexels and grab a free photo - any photo you like - and save it to your computer.

**The How-To:**

1. Go to Pexels.com

2. Scroll through the new photos (updated daily) or use the search bar

3. Click on the image you want to use

4. Choose from the various download options (click the drop-down arrow beside "free download" for size options) & save to your computer

Pexels has the same Creative Commons Zero license that Unsplash uses, which means these photographs are free for you to use, alter, edit, and publish anywhere, however you'd like, without giving credit to the photographer.

We'll do one more piece of photo-collecting prep work tomorrow (and I'll share with you a paid photo site I love, as well as my pros & cons for using these sites)!

# Day 3 – Phone Fun

Isn't Pexels a fun site? I hope you were able to find at least one image you felt would work well on your blog or website.

Yep, that's right. Did you know that the images you're finding should reflect your blog and social media brand as much as the topic of your blog post or quote? As you continue to build up an image library, think about the colors that you already use on your blog, the types of photos you want to use:

- Outdoor
- Indoor
- People
- Animals
- Abstract

...and the feel you want readers to experience:

- Light
- Inviting
- Dark
- Serious
- Playful
- Whimsical

This is how you will begin to develop a recognizable, consistent brand on social media and your blog. The more focused your images, graphics, fonts, and voice are on all your platforms, the easier it will be for your audience to relate and engage with you, wherever they find you!


**Today's Challenge**:

Grab your phone - or your camera - and snap a few of your photos that work with the style and feel of your site.

While I love Unsplash and Pexels, there's honestly nothing better than using your photos if you can.

On the one hand, free and paid image sites will give you the option of hundreds of photos to choose from - which is perfect if you want a photo of a woman walking through an open field in the spring, and it's currently the depths of winter where you live.

But the downside? If you find a photo you love on those sites, it's only a matter of time before you see it appearing on other blogs and social media sites, too.

The only way to avoid that? Use photos you've taken! Even just using your phone (which is how I snap most of my photos) you can create a library of images that not only represent you and your style but will already fit into your brand - because they're yours.

I've found David Molnar's "iPhone Only Photography" book and course to be extremely helpful if you want to enhance your smartphone photography.

Tomorrow we'll jump over to one of my favorite sites, and we'll put those photos you've found in a safe place!

# Day 4 – Uploading to Canva

Are you ready to do something with those photos you've been finding this week? We're not going to create any graphics with them quite yet, but we're going to get them set up today on my favorite site!

**Today's Challenge:**

Upload your photos to Canva!

**The How-To:**

1. Go to www.canva.com

2. Sign in, or if you're new to Canva, set up your free account

3. Pause :: **Don't get overwhelmed**. There are a lot of options when you get into Canva, and I promise we'll walk through all of them. Don't panic!

4. Click on "Social Media" at the top of the page, under "Create a Design"

5. Ignore all the pretty templates (so hard! I know!) and click "Uploads" on the left sidebar

6. Click the green "Upload Your Own Images" button and add the images you've been saving to your computer this week

## FAQs

**Q: Why won't my photo upload? It's just spinning.**

A: Large images from some of the sites we've visited sometimes save in a file size that is too large for Canva to handle. If you run into that problem, you can use your favorite tool to resize the image if you already know how to do that, or do what I do and use PicMonkey.

Go to PicMonkey.com, upload your image, and click "Resize" (it will be on the bottom left when your image opens). Change the width dimension – the first box – to 900. The height dimension should automatically change to keep the original image proportion correct. Click "save" and save the resized image to your desktop (and rename it, so you know it's the smaller version). Now you should be able to upload to Canva with no problem!

**Q: Can I upload multiple images at a time?**

A: Technically, yes. As long as the images are all small enough you can hold down the CTRL key and select several files at one time. However, Canva sometimes gets overwhelmed when you do that and forgets to upload one or freezes. If you have the time, uploading one-by-one is the best practice for this exercise.

That's it! No need to save - Canva does that for you. And there are some other brilliant features to this site that we'll get into in a few days - but rest easy knowing your images are safe and sound and waiting for you!

Tomorrow we'll talk fonts! Woot!

# Day 5 – Fonts!

One of the easiest ways to take your graphic or text from "eh" to "amazing" is to limit the number of fonts you put in front of your reader's eye. They want to know where to look, and fonts are your way of telling them READ THIS FIRST.

**Today's Challenge:**

Choose 2-3 fonts to use throughout the challenge.

Just 2 or 3? But there are hundreds of font options, and they're all so pretty, and wouldn't it be better if I used more?

**Lean in, friend. When it comes to chocolate, more is more. When it comes to fonts? Less is more.**

Maybe you already have a font family on your blog design that you love and want to use (mine is Lato, for example), and that's great.

**Consistency creates brand awareness!**

But if you're thinking of fonts for the first time, consider choosing one or two sans serif fonts (fonts that appear plain, with no short lines across the top and bottom of the letters, like Arial – the font used in this book) and one serif font (a font with short lines across the top and bottom of the letters, like American Typewriter), or a font that looks like handwriting, like Allura.

You'll be totally set up for success, AND you'll have a beautiful fancy font to use when you want to call out certain words or phrases as we jump into some quote creation next week (it's coming soon! I promise!).

Need help finding fonts? Head over to Canva and browse through some of the pre-created templates - when you click on the text it will tell you which font is used!

Or if you want to have a lot of fun and browse a ton of options, you can check out Google Fonts, where you can sort the options by Serif, Sans Serif, Handwriting, and more!

And feel free to be inspired by Pinterest - take a look at the images you've pinned and shared and think about why you love the design and try to find similar fonts to use in your graphics.

Tomorrow we'll finish up our graphic design "mise en place"!

# Day 6 – Quotable Quotes

You have stuck with me through the tedious prep work! Woot! Today is the last day we'll spend getting our thoughts and details organized, and tomorrow we'll get to create!

But before we do that, we need one last item. We have the images. We have the fonts. Now we need the words!

**Today's Challenge:**

Make a list of quotes (famous quotes, Scriptures, your awesome content from your blog) to use later this week.

Whether we're making text-only images, quote graphics, or printables, one thing is a "must have" - words! Open a Google Drive doc or Word Doc and start collecting your favorite quotes and phrases.

Maybe there is a Scripture that you'd love to share with your social media followers or a key phrase from one of your recent blog posts that you'd like to put on Facebook - write them down!

Unlike fonts, when it comes to quotes, the more, the merrier! But if you're in a time crunch today, I'd suggest finding at least four quotes. Try to find some that are shorter - think "tweet" length (around 140 characters or one short sentence) for now. When we get to the printable creation part of the course, we'll have room for more text!

Tomorrow we'll create our first graphic using one of my favorite apps!

# Day 7 – Text Only Graphics: Rhonna

It's time to create!!

Here's how we're going to work through the next 24 days - we're going to spend ten days working on text-only graphics, which means you won't be using any of those gorgeous images you found quite yet. We're going to refine our skills in adding text to a background in several formats first so that we can get comfortable with that, and then we'll jump up to the next level.

Then we'll spend ten days working on various image editing and quote graphic challenges, followed by two days of creating very specific social media images, and then wrap it up with a printable.

Sounds good? Let's get to it! You'll be a pro in no time!

**Today's Challenge:**

Create a text-only graphic using the Rhonna app

**Disclosure**: The apps referenced in this book are for use on an iPhone, so if you're on something else, I'm so sorry. Many of them are also available on Andriod phones, but you might need to find alternatives occasionally.

Also, while I usually only use the free version of most apps and websites, the $1.99 for this one is well worth it!

**The How To:**

1. Download the Rhonna app from the App Store or Google Play

2. Click on the red image icon on the left

3. Choose a plain background from the options included in the app

4. Tap the blue checkmark when you've found one you like

5. Click on the "T" on top left side of the screen and choose a font pack (you can change your fonts any time)

6. Double tap the text box to enter your quote and click "done"

7. You can scroll through various font and color options, move the quote around on the screen by dragging the text box or change the size by pushing or pulling the little circle on the bottom right corner of the text box

8. When you're ready to save, click the blue square with three white lines on the top right and choose "share" – you can pick the size you want for your image and save it to your camera roll


Tomorrow we'll do a little work on one of my other favorite websites - PicMonkey!

# Day 8 – Text Only Graphics – PicMonkey

So how'd you do yesterday? Were you able to create an image using the Rhonna app? There are so many great options available to create beautiful quote graphics on your phone that it was hard for me to pick just one, but hopefully, that one was pretty easy to figure out!

**Today's Challenge:**

Create a text-only graphic using PicMonkey

Before we get into this one, I want you to know that I just flat don't know how to use anything fancy like Photoshop. And if you do, you have skills that are beyond me!

Everything I've learned to do on my blog has happened in PicMonkey, Canva or some combination of the two!

**The How-To:**

1. Go to PicMonkey.com

2. Click on "design" to open a design template

3. Click on the "textures" icon in the left sidebar (it looks like a blue crisscross pattern) to choose a background design

4. Click "apply" when you've found one you like (I like the chalkboard designs under "Boards" personally)

5. Click "Tt" in the left sidebar to add text to the background (tip: click the "add text" button first, type your quote" then go back and change the fonts later - you'll need to play around a bit to figure out what works best)

6. When you like how it looks, click "save" and save it to your desktop!

## A few hints:

- To change the font or color of just one word in your quote, double-click the word, then choose the font style
- If your 2 or 3 fonts from day 5 are on your computer, you can use them in PicMonkey by clicking "Yours" to access your fonts
- If you happen to see something you want to use, but it has a "crown" icon on it, it means you need to have a Royale (paid) subscription to the site to use it

## FAQ

**Q: If I want to share this image on Instagram, can I upload from my computer?**

A: Unfortunately, no. Instagram doesn't allow you to upload your images directly from your computer without using a third-party tool (see Day 23 for my favorite option). If you'd rather not learn to use another tool, you can simply open your email, attach your image and email it to yourself. Open your email on your phone, click on the image and save it to your photo file. Then simply open Instagram and upload your image and caption!

Tomorrow we'll jump back over to Canva and learn how to use one of their beautiful templates!

# Day 9 – Text Only Facebook Graphic – Canva

Isn't PicMonkey so fun? It offers so many wonderful free image creation tools - but in case you didn't notice, they also have some fabulous paid tools for their "Royale" members. I've paid for those before and - if at the end of this - PicMonkey is your website of choice, then I HIGHLY recommend it.

But today we're going to head back over to our buddy Canva. Even though you already have some great photos waiting there for you, we're going to spend some more time working just with fonts & quotes today!

### Today's Challenge:

Create a text-only Facebook graphic using a Canva template

### The How-To:

1. Go to canva.com

2. Login if you aren't still connected, then click on "Facebook Post"

3. Scroll through the designs until you've found a free template you like - it'll be marked "free" in the bottom right corner (you can choose one that costs money, but I happen to prefer "free")

4. Click the template you want to use to bring it up on the page

5. Click on the text you want to edit, and enter your quote

6. When you like how it looks, click "download" and save it to your desktop as an image!

**A few hints:**

- To change the font, size or color use the dropdowns that appear at the top of the page when you click on the text.
- Canva doesn't allow you to change just one word in your quote as easily as PicMonkey, so you'll need to start a new text box (for now, just click "copy" from the editing menu that appears to make life easy) and format those words separately.

Tomorrow we'll be back in Canva to try one of their other templates!

# Day 10 – Text Only Instagram Graphic – Canva

You are doing such an excellent job. I mean it. It's so fun to see your creativity, and I love that you've been brave enough to try this with me! If you have an image you've created that you want me to see, just use the #creativebasics hashtag on Instagram!

We're heading back to Canva today for another little template challenge to get you used to the features and options that are available. By the time we get to the part where you're designing with your images, you'll be a ROCK STAR at these basics!

**Today's Challenge:**

Create a text-only Instagram graphic using a Canva template

**The How-To:**

1. Go to canva.com

2. Log in if you aren't still connected, then click on the plus sign to view more templates and choose "Instagram Post"

3. Scroll through the designs until you've found a free template you like - it'll be marked "free" in the bottom right corner (you can choose one that costs money, but I happen to prefer "free")

4. Click the template you want to use to bring it up on the page

5. Click on the text you want to edit, and enter your quote

6. When you like how it looks, click "download" and save it to your desktop as an image!

**A few hints:**

- To change the font, size or color use the dropdowns that appear at the top of the page when you click on the text.
- Canva doesn't allow you to change just one word in your quote as easily as PicMonkey, so you'll need to start a new text box (for now, just click "copy" from the editing menu that appears to make life easy) and format those words separately.
- Have you noticed that Canva has these templates already at the ideal size for you, so you don't have to change anything when you share it online? I love that!

Need help using Instagram? They have a fabulous "help" section that can answer almost all of your questions!

Tomorrow we'll be back in Canva to wrap up this little section on creating text-only images using templates!

# Day 11 – Text Only Blog Graphic – Canva

I know it can be a little hard to keep up with these daily challenges, so hopefully you've realized that they're easy enough that you can do more than one each day if you need to catch up (or, if you need to skip one, that's ok, too! You'll still learn a BUNCH by the end of this series!).

We're spending some more time at Canva today, so let's get to it!

**Today's Challenge:**

Create a text-only blog graphic using a Canva template.

**The How-To:**

1. Go to canva.com

2. Login if you aren't still connected, then click on "Blog Graphic"

3. Scroll through the designs until you've found a free template you like - it'll be marked "free" in the bottom right corner (you can choose one that costs money, but I happen to prefer "free")

4. Click the template you want to use to bring it up on the page

5. Click on the text you want to edit, and enter your quote

6. When you like how it looks, click "download" and save it to your desktop as an image!

One of my favorite parts of the templates under "Blogging & eBooks" is the ability to create easy infographics! These are perfect if you need a visual representation of a process, a recipe, or a timeline - and they're already set up and ready for you - and they look great on Pinterest.

You can choose new icons or images by clicking on "Elements" on the left sidebar.

You can either search for a specific image or browse through the options by scrolling down the page.

Tomorrow we'll be back in Canva - but we'll say goodbye to templates!

# Day 12 – Text Only Graphic – Canva

Grab a cup of coffee and let's get to this one!

**Today's Challenge:**

Create a text-only graphic in Canva - using your design!

That's right - today it's up to you to choose which style you want to start with (Facebook, Instagram, or Blog Graphic) and create your very own text graphic. We still won't be adding any of our images quite yet but the background, quote and font style are totally up to you!

**The How-To:**

1. Go to canva.com

2. Login if you aren't still connected, then click on the format you'd like to use (click "more" to view additional options)

3. Click "background" in the left sidebar to choose your background style (you can change the color using the options at the top - click the plus sign if you don't see the color you want)

4. Click "Text" in the left sidebar to open the text editor - and choose one of the "add text" options

5. Enter your quote, adding other text fields as needed and having fun with the fonts, size, and color

6. When you like how it looks, click "download" and save it to your desktop as an image!

Tomorrow we'll be back in Canva to learn how to overlays to help our text pop.

# Day 13 – Text Only Graphic  Using Overlays – Canva

It's good to see you again, friend! I hope you're enjoying this course and learning a few new things!

**Today's Challenge:**

Create a text-only graphic in Canva - using shape overlays!

I feel like you just looked at me with a question mark in your eyes. Shape overlays are the shapes and banners you often see on quote images that contain the quote and make the text pop. This is a super useful tool when we start using images since our text can sometimes get lost on a busy background!

**The How-To:**

1. Go to canva.com

2. Login if you aren't still connected, then click on the image format you'd like to use

3. Click "background" in the left sidebar to choose your background style (you can change the color using the options at the top - click the plus sign if you don't see the color you want)

4. Click "Elements" in the left sidebar to open the text editor

5. Type "text holder" into the search bar

6. Click on the one you like best to add it to your background

7. Enter your quote, adding other text fields as needed and having fun with the fonts, size, and color - keep in mind you might need to find a different text holder to fit the length of your quote. Shape overlays in Canva are created to auto-resize your text to fit the size of the text holder.

8. When you like how it looks, click "download" and save it to your desktop as an image!

Tomorrow we'll be back in Canva to learn how to make our fonts work for us!

# Day 14 – Text Only Graphic Fonts – Canva

Have you ever tried to make a quote image and couldn't quite figure out how to get the font size, spacing, or transparency exactly right? It's hard enough trying to decide which fonts to use, and then when they don't work the right way it can be even more frustrating!

Never fear - we'll figure this one out together!

**Today's Challenge:**

Create a text-only graphic in Canva - changing the font spacing & transparency.

**The How-To:**

1. Go to canva.com

2. Log in if you aren't still connected, then click on one of the text images you've already created that Canva has saved for you (you can edit or reuse those any time!)

3. Click the text you want to edit

4. From the editing menu at the top of the page, choose "text spacing"

5. Play time! Look at what happens when you make the text closer together or further apart until you like what you have – letter spacing moves the individual letters and line spacing moves the space between the lines of text

6. Now click on the button beside "Arrange" - the series of faded boxes - to adjust the transparency

7. Slide the bar around until your text has the faded look you think looks best - this works especially well for watermarks (we'll get to those) and if you want a softer look to your text

8. When you like how it looks, click "download" and save it to your desktop as an image!


Different spacing gives the text a different feel - and these tools can be especially helpful when we're trying to fit text onto a busy photo or if a little less space between the words conveys the feeling you're looking for with your quote.

Tomorrow we'll be back in Canva to make one last text-only image before we get back to those gorgeous images that have been patiently waiting for us since Day 4.

# Day 15 – Text Only Pinterest Graphic - Canva

We're almost there!

You have done a fantastic job making some really beautiful text-only images, and today we'll make our last one! We're halfway through the course, can you believe it?

Tomorrow we'll get back to those images you found in our first week together, but for today? It's time to play with Pinterest!

**Today's Challenge:**

Create a text-only Pinterest graphic in Canva.

**The How-To:**

1. Go to canva.com

2. Login if you aren't still connected, click "More" and scroll until you find the Pinterest template

3. Find a free template you want to use and add your quote

4. You've totally got this! Use all those font/style/size/spacing/transparency tricks we've learned over the last two weeks to create a beautiful Pinterest image.

5. When you like how it looks, click "download" and save it to your desktop as an image!

It's a perfect, pinnable image! Pinterest loves tall, vertical images, so I like how easy it is to make these in Canva. If you happen to have a square image created for Instagram or Facebook, you can add it to a Pinterest layout (either using one that already has a spot for an image or adding an image frame to a plain layout), add a little extra text or a border, and POOF! Awesome, right?

Tomorrow we'll be back in Canva to learn how to add those watermarks to the photos we've already saved!

# Day 16 – Watermarks

Remember those images you found on Unsplash, Pexels and your phone? It's time to do a little work with them today! That's right - this is the start of the section of the course that focuses on images - woot!

**Today's Challenge:**

Create a watermark on your images in Canva.

**The How-To:**

1. Go to canva.com

2. Login if you aren't still connected and choose the Instagram post template, just to make it easier when you share later!

3. Scroll all the way down until you find a blank template already set up to hold one image – click to select it.

4. Click "Uploads" in the left sidebar to choose one of the photos you've already uploaded - drag and drop it over onto the Instagram post square

**Note**: If the image place-keeper is missing on your template Canva won't automatically fill your image to fit the space.

5. Click "Text" in the left sidebar to add text to your image (I choose "add a little bit of body text" for watermarks because you want a small font)

6. Use the editing tools to change the font, size, and transparency (I go with a 14 point font or smaller for a watermark, and I decrease the transparency to around 90%)

7. When you like how it looks, click "download" and save it to your desktop as an image!

So what's the big deal about adding your website or watermark to your images? If you are creating beautiful quote images, they'll probably be shared. And when they're shared, they might not be linked back to your original blog post, or even your account.

BUT if you have your name, website, or other identifying watermark on your image, readers will be able to find their way back to you (and it gives you proper credit for creating the image!). It is extremely important to give credit to the original author or creator when you share someone else's work.

**Bonus Tip:** If you have a signature or logo that you'd rather use as your watermark, using PicMonkey is the easiest way to add those to your images. Simply:

1. Go to PicMonkey

2. Click "Edit" and upload your image

3. On the left sidebar, click the butterfly icon to access the overlays, and choose "Add Your Own"

4. Upload your logo/signature image, adjust the size, and use the "fade" feature to adjust the transparency

5. Save it to your desktop and tada! All done :)

Tomorrow we'll spend a little time in PicMonkey learning to create collages!

# Day 17 – Photo Collage – PicMonkey

Raising my cup of coffee to you today, friends!

{Insert happy dance}

Today we're going to create a photo collage. Which might not seem like something you'll use very often, but if you ever host a giveaway on your blog, want to create a great Pinterest graphic using photos from a party, or you simply want to do a roundup of your favorite things, collages can make your content pop!


**Today's Challenge:**

Create a photo collage in PicMonkey.


**The How-To:**

1. Go to PicMonkey

2. Click on "Collage" and then "Add Images" to choose the 3-5 photos you want to include (you can either do cmd+click on a Mac or ctrl+click on a PC to choose multiple photos at once, or you can upload one at a time - you can always add more photos later by repeating the same steps.

3. Drag and drop your photos into the template OR choose a different template by clicking on the icon with three squares and choosing the one that works best for your photos

4. Move the image boxes around to find the best fit for your photos (you can also add and delete image boxes to customize your collage - to add one, simply drag a new photo onto the collage. To delete one, just click the "x" in the upper right corner.)

5. When you like how it looks, change the size (I prefer 600 wide instead of 2000 - it just looks better on my blog & takes up less space) and save it!

**Bonus Tip:** You can, of course, also create collages in Canva with some of their fun layouts. The process is similar - choose the template you like, upload your photos, and drag & drop!

I happen to think PicMonkey makes editing/cropping your images a little easier, but both tools are great (and now that you're becoming pros at using both sites, you can have fun playing to figure out what works best for you!).

Tomorrow we'll do part 2 of our collage creation using another one of my favorite apps!

# Day 18 – Photo Collage – MixGram

So we've already played a little on Rhonna to create some text-only images, and today I'm introducing you to my favorite collage creation app – MixGram!

Sometimes you have photos on your phone that you want to share (maybe you want to do a "Follow Friday" series on Instagram, for example), and you want to show them off in a collage, but you don't want to email them to yourself, make the collage in PicMonkey or Canva, email it back to yourself, and then upload to Instagram.

MixGram has great collage layouts, and I love how creative you can get with them! Plus, it couldn't be easier to use! The free version does have a lot of ads, but they don't bother me enough to pay for the full version.

**Today's Challenge:**

Create a photo collage in MixGram.

**The How-To:**

1. Add MixGram to your phone (again, I have an iPhone, so if you have something else I'm so sorry if the steps don't match)

2. Click on one of the gray boxes in the design to add photos to your collage – MixGram will automatically put your images into the layout for you

3. You can easily swap out images if you need to rearrange them

4. Add text, emojis, or edit the size of the collage design by using the tools at the bottom of the screen

5. Save your image and either post immediately to Twitter, Instagram, Facebook, or save to your camera roll

Fun and easy, right? Be sure to take some time to play with MixGram when you have a moment - you can't break it, and if you don't like what you create you can always start over!

**Bonus Tip**: If you want to create a collage that includes a video, I like the VidStich app. Super easy to use, free, and a fun way to combine photos and video into one collage!

Tomorrow we'll head back over to Canva and learn about some of their great photo editing tools!

# Day 19 – Photo Filters – Canva

We're keeping it pretty simple today so you can catch up later if you need to.

Even though this challenge won't take long, learning how to use the image filter options in Canva will be a tremendous tool for you when we start creating quote images.

So let's get to it!

**Today's Challenge:**

Turn one of your photos black & white using the filter tools in Canva.

**The How-To:**

1. Head over to Canva and choose the Instagram post template

2. Scroll WAY down through the templates until you find the one set up with one image holder and click to choose it

3. Click "Uploads" in the left sidebar and drag and drop your photo onto the template

4. Click on your photo and then choose "Filter" from the top toolbar

5. Click the arrows until you find "grayscale."

6. Feel free to add a watermark to your photo before you click "Download" and save

Learning to use the filters in Canva - or any photo editing tool - will help you create quote graphics that are unique and on-brand.

This is the section that will allow you adjust the amount of brightness in your photo to help your text pop. It's also where (under "Advanced Options") you can blur the image to help your reader focus on your text.

Just because we find great photos online (or take great photos!) doesn't mean we don't sometimes have to make little changes to help it fit our style, work with our text, or just look awesome!

Tomorrow we'll head back over to PicMonkey to create our first quote graphic! WOOT!!

# Day 20 – Quote Image – PicMonkey

Day 20!!
Can you believe we only have ten more days? I can't thank you enough for sticking this out with me and doing these challenges. It's been so fun!

We're going to get started today making some quote images, and I'm so excited for you to use all those tools and tricks we've learned the last 19 days to rock this one!

I'm not going to go into all the detail about where to find the tools & how to use them since we've already covered that part, but flip back if you need to reference any of the steps.

**Today's Challenge:**

Create a quote image in PicMonkey.

**The How-To:**

1. Go to PicMonkey and click "Edit" to choose the photo you want to use (choose one of the ones you found in our first few days together)

2. Click "Tt" in the sidebar to add text

3. Adjust the font, size, and transparency (don't forget to add your watermark, and feel free to play with text overlays!)

4. Click "Save" (keeping in mind you might want to resize the photo before you save, so it isn't a gigantic file)

**Can I tell you a secret?**

I almost never get the right look on an image the first time. I get an idea, or find inspiration on Pinterest and try it out. Sometimes it takes me a few tries to get the fonts sized the right way, or I need to scrap an idea for a text overlay because it's just not working.

The trick is to keep trying! The more often you make these graphics, the more you'll refine your specific "look" - and that will make it easier for you each time you do a new one!

Tomorrow I'll show you how to do something fun in PicMonkey that I just love.

# Day 21 – Shape Cutouts – PicMonkey

I wish we could all share cupcakes with extra sprinkles today before we get started. Grab a cup of coffee and let's get into today's challenge, which I think is a fun feature of PicMonkey and something I've had trouble figuring out how to do for a long time.

**Today's Challenge:**

Create a circle graphic using the shape cutouts in PicMonkey.

**The How-To:**

1. Go to PicMonkey and click "Edit" to choose the photo you want to use (choose one of the ones you found in our first few days together)

2. Click on the "Frames" icon in the left sidebar

3. Choose "Shape Cutouts" at the top - it will automatically choose the circle for you (but if you're feeling sassy you can totally choose a different shape!)

4. Drag the circle on your photo around until you like what you see - this is what your final image will look like (if you want it to be a smaller circle, use the size slider in the editor on the left)

5. Click "Apply" and then feel free to either leave it as is and save or add text first.

6. Click "Save" when you're finished!

So fun, right?

Make sure you check back in tomorrow because we're going to head back to Canva!

# Day 22 – Facebook Quote Graphic – Canva

Today is the part of the course I think most of you were waiting for - spending a few days making quote graphics in Canva!

Let's get to it, shall we?

**Today's Challenge:**

Create a quote graphic in Canva using a Facebook post template.

**The How-To:**

1. Go to Canva and choose "Facebook Post" - this is already set up to be the preferred size for images to be shared with your audience on Facebook

2. Choose a template that you'd like to use, keeping in mind that you might need to delete or replace some of the "paid" features if you don't want to ... you know ... pay for them

3. Head to "Uploads" to drag and drop your photo onto the background (just an FYI: Canva will automatically apply the template filter settings to your photo, so you might need to change those if you don't like how it looks)

4. Click on the text you want to edit and add one of your quotes you've been collecting - you can keep the font formatting in the template, or adjust it to fit your font preferences

5. When you like how it looks, click "download" and save as an image to your desktop!

I can't wait to see what you've created today!

Tomorrow we'll be back in Canva, this time to work with an Instagram template.

# Day 23 – Instagram Quote Graphic – Canva

Can you believe we only have a week left? The amount of work you've done is simply amazing, and I hope each lesson leaves you feeling a little more confident in your abilities to make beautiful social media graphics!

As we get into today's challenge, I want to encourage you to think about the space your text takes up on your image. Often when I'm creating a quote image and can't figure out why it's not looking right, it's because I'm either making the text too large and it's overwhelming the photo, or the text is too small and getting lost.

Don't be afraid to leave some space around your text, to move it from one side to the other, or to use different sizes of the same font to help direct your reader's eye!

**Today's Challenge:**

Create a quote graphic in Canva using an Instagram post template.

**The How-To:**

1. Go to Canva and choose "Instagram Post" - this is already set up to be the preferred size for images to be shared with your audience on Instagram

2. Choose a template that you'd like to use, keeping in mind that you might need to delete or replace some of the "paid" features if you don't want to ... you know ... pay for them

3. Head to "Uploads" to drag and drop your photo onto the background (just an FYI: Canva will automatically apply the template filter settings to your photo, so you might need to change those if you don't like how it looks)

4. Click on the text you want to edit and add one of your quotes you've been collecting - you can keep the font formatting in the template, or adjust it to fit your font preferences

5. When you like how it looks, click "download" and save as an image to your desktop!

*You can do shape cutouts in Canva, too - just find the right template!*

**Bonus Tip**: There aren't many great tools for scheduling Instagram posts, but one that I've found and like a lot is Later. You'll create an account on the website, add the app to your phone and then follow the very easy directions to upload your image (must be at least 610 x 610), add a caption, and schedule your post. Be sure to turn on notifications on the app because it will send you a message when it's time to post your image!

Creating Instagram images in Canva will ensure that your images are the right size (and shape!) for Instagram, and then you can use Later to upload, schedule and post!

Tomorrow we'll be back in Canva, and we're going to get creative!

# Day 24 – Quote Graphic – Canva

I'm excited to see what everyone designs today. Be sure to share on Instagram with the #creativebasics hashtag! We've figured out how to format fonts, edit photos with filters, use overlays and text holders and now it's your turn to create something that is genuinely YOU.

No templates, no rules, just whatever you think looks best using the skills you already have. Ready?

**Today's Challenge:**

Create a quote graphic in Canva - anything goes!

**The How-To:**

1. Head over to Canva

2. Create whatever you want!

3. When you love it, download & save the image to your computer.

**Bonus Tip**: Here's what I love about a tool like Canva. Once you've created an image that you like, it's saved for you to edit and use as many times as you want!

Tomorrow we'll be back in Canva to make Pinterest graphics!

# Day 25 – Pinterest Quote Graphic – Canva

Did you have fun yesterday? As much as I love learning something new, I feel like I don't absorb it until I'm left on my own to play and create.

Although in school I remember hating the "freedom" to write about any topic I wanted, so hopefully yesterday was fun and not stressful.

I'm just going to pretend you all loved it, ok? Okay.

Today we're going to jump back into using a Canva template to create a quote image for Pinterest. You might remember making a text-only image for Pinterest on Day 15, and today we're going to take it up a level by using one of our images!

**Today's Challenge:**

Create a quote graphic in Canva using a Pinterest template!

I'm not going to walk you through the steps because I think you've figured it out by now! Just start with a Pinterest template that you like and add your photo, quote, and font styles, keeping in mind that you can always use the image filters and text holders to help you text pop (you can go back to some of the previous sections for reminders on how to use those).

You don't need to totally reinvent the wheel if you have a graphic you already like! Consider using one of your Instagram or Facebook images and adding some extra content above or below to help make it more compelling (and the right size) for Pinterest.

Tomorrow I'm going to share with you a trick to making sharing non-square images on Instagram a breeze!

# Day 26 – Instagram Cropping

Today is another easy challenge day (in case you want to catch up tomorrow) but it was, surprisingly, the tip that attendees at a conference said was their favorite takeaway of a 3-hour graphics lab. Are you ready?

**Today's Challenge:**

Use Instagram's cropping tool to share a non-square image.

**The How-To:**

1. Open Instagram

2. Choose a photo from your phone that isn't a square

3. In the bottom left corner of your image click the cropping tool circle

4. Click "next" and post as usual!

That's it! No more frustration over Instagram chopping your images off, losing your watermark, or trying to figure out which friend to crop out of the photo before you share. You can also use an app called Squaready if you prefer, but using the native Instagram tool cuts out a few extra steps.

Tomorrow we're going to use the skills we've been learning to give our Facebook pages a little makeover ;)

# Day 27 – Facebook Cover – Canva

We are wrapping up this course with our last section of challenges, and we're going to do a few things that will take the tools we've learned and use them to give our social media spaces a little makeover.

**Today's Challenge:**

Create a Facebook Cover in Canva.

**The How-To:**

1. Head to Canva

2. Click on "more" and find the "Facebook Cover" template

3. Find a design you like, or make one from scratch (whatever makes you happy!)

4. Add your photos and text, make your edits, and "download" to save to your computer

5. Don't forget to upload it to your Facebook page!

I've tried making Facebook cover images in other tools, and they never seem to line up just right.

**A few hints:** you'll want to ensure your text falls closer to the center and bottom of your image, and you'll want to leave some space around your text to make sure nothing is chopped off accidentally by a random Facebook cropping incident.

If you don't have a Facebook page (I have more fun on Twitter and Instagram), you can use the photo collage templates to share recent photos on your personal Facebook page.

If you have a page for your blog or website, however, using Canva is a great way to create cover images that match your branding on your text and quote images!

Speaking of Twitter, tomorrow we'll be back to give our Twitter profiles a makeover!

# Day 28 – Twitter Header – Canva

I heard a rumor that your Twitter page is feeling a little neglected now that you've given your Facebook page a bit of a makeover. Fortunately for us, Canva has a tool and a template for almost anything we'd want to do - including Twitter Headers!

**Today's Challenge:**

Create a Twitter Header in Canva.

**The How-To:**

1. Head to Canva

2. Click on "more" and find the "Twitter Header" template

3. Find a design you like, or make one from scratch (whatever makes you happy!)

4. Add your photos and text, make your edits, and "download" to save to your computer

5. Don't forget to upload it to your Twitter page!

You might be wondering why you couldn't just upload the Facebook Cover image as your Twitter Header.

Well, depending on your design, it might work. But unfortunately for us, Facebook and Twitter like to be JUST different enough that the sizes, location of our avatar, and general spacing sometimes make it challenging to use one image in two places.

**Bonus Tip**: Consistency in your brand is key, which means keeping a similar look and feel to your avatars and header images across your social media platforms, and make sure your bio is consistent as well!

See you tomorrow!

# Day 29 – Upgrade Time!

Sniffle.

I won't be sad that we end our time together tomorrow. Nope.

SNIFFLE.

**Today's Challenge:**

Update one of your first text-only images in Canva.

**The How-To:**

1. Head to Canva

2. Find one of your first text-only images and give it a makeover!

3. When you're happy with how it looks, click "Download" and save as an image to your computer.

Why go back and update one of your first images? The same reason we go back and update our evergreen content with new links on our blogs, or why we redesign our blogs or take new headshots.

We're always learning, always growing, and refreshing archived graphics is a great way to give your content new life on social media!

Tomorrow we'll do our final challenge together - creating a printable!

# Day 30 – Printable – Canva

You did it!! This is it - our last day together, and I can't tell you how much fun I've had. I hope you've enjoyed our time together and that you've learned at least one thing you didn't know before - that will make it totally worth it in my book!

We're going to end our course with what I've lovingly termed our "final" project - just like in college; we're going to take all we've learned and put it together into one gorgeous, beautiful, PRINTABLE!

And yes, I'll even share some tools you can use to share your printable with your audience once you've created it.

**Today's Challenge:**

Create a printable in Canva.

**The How-To:**

1. Head to Canva

2. Click on "more" and find the "Real Estate Flyer" template (because it's already sized to be 8.5 x 11, which is what you'll want)

3. Choose a layout if one will work for you, or start with a blank image holder template

4. Drag & drop your desired background image from your Uploads, or choose a background

5. Add your text, using overlays and various text sizes that work well with your quote and brand

6. When you like how it looks, add your watermark, and download to your computer as a PDF

This will probably be your most time-consuming project that we've done. It takes me awhile to find the right combination of font sizes and design to match my quote - but I find that checking out printables I've already added to my Pinterest boards helps a lot. Not to copy, but for inspiration.

Here are some things to ask yourself when you're looking at a printable someone else created that you like a lot:

- What is it about the fonts that I like?
- How did they use size to add interest?
- Are there other design elements I could add?
- How many colors do they use in their design?

Maybe all of your favorite printables are chalkboard art - that's a pretty clear direction to go in for yours! Or maybe you like hand lettering, or you prefer a shorter quote in large blocky letters. Whatever it is that you try, just don't be afraid to start! You can always start over!

Once your printable is saved to your computer, there are a few ways you can share it with your readers. You can save it to your Google Drive or Dropbox and share the link with your readers, or you could use a WordPress tool called "Easy Digital Downloads."

I love this tool, and it's a great way to control not only your free content (and track downloads) but also gives you the opportunity to sell products in the future, in case you ever have an eBook or set of printables that you want to offer you, readers.

You'll also have a clear link to share with your email subscribers if a free printable is something you'd like to gift them when they sign up!

{high five}

You did it!!

# Bonus Material: YouTube Thumbnails

You didn't think I'd leave you without a little bonus material, did you? I've added a few more frequently used templates here at the end, in case you breezed through the last 30 days and wanted something extra to do! It's like extra credit – awesome to have, but entirely optional!

**Today's Bonus:**

Create a YouTube Thumbnail image in Canva.

**The How-To:**

1. Go to Canva and click on the "plus" sign to find and select "YouTube Thumbnail"

2. Choose a template that you'd like to use, keeping in mind that you might need to delete or replace some of the "paid" features if you don't want to ... you know ... pay for them

3. Head to "Uploads" to drag and drop your photo onto the background (just an FYI: Canva will automatically apply the template filter settings to your photo, so you might need to change those if you don't like how it looks)

4. Click on the text you want to edit and add the name of your YouTube video or channel here

5. When you like how it looks, click "download" and save as an image to your desktop!

Often when we upload videos to YouTube, the thumbnail images they select for us are – shall we say – unflattering. Creating and uploading a custom YouTube thumbnail not only avoids the awkward "half blinking half talking what am I doing with my hands" pose, but it gives you the opportunity to brand your YouTube videos.

# Bonus Material: Ripl

Creating a video for your social media channels can be a fun way to engage your audience. Facebook loves the video that is uploaded natively to your page, while Instagram only allows you to show off 15 precious seconds of your video. And it loops it endlessly, so how do you choose which clips to share?

Today we're going to play with one of my new favorite apps – Ripl! Ripl creates GIF and short videos using still images and your captions – perfect for advertising an upcoming event, inviting friends to a book club, or just taking your quote graphics to the next level.

**Today's Bonus:**

Create a video in Ripl.

**The How-To:**

1. Download the free Ripl app in the iTunes store (there are in-app purchases available, but I use the free version)

2. Choose an image from your phone's camera roll if you'd like, or leave that blank & you'll be able to choose from a variety of preset backgrounds on the next screen

3. Enter your main caption and any secondary text you'd like to include (you can go back to this page later if you need to make changes)

4. Click the arrow at the top right to choose the animated layout you prefer for your graphic (you can move the overlays, change colors, fonts, and sizes to find what works best for your image)

5. When you like how it looks, click the arrow at the top right to share on Facebook, Instagram, or save to your camera roll.

# Bonus Material: Word Swag

The $4.99 for this one is well worth it because of the beautiful way they allow me to add metallic fonts to my designs. I've even used this app to create the design for my Holy Hustle apparel!

**Today's Bonus:**

Create a graphic in Word Swag.

**The How To:**
1. Download the Word Swap app from the App Store or Google Play
2. Click on the photo icon on the bottom right when the screen opens
3. Choose a plain background from the options included in the app by clicking on the one you'd like to use
4. Click on the "Crop" button (it should be pre-set to a square crop, perfect for Instagram)
5. Double tap where it says "double tap me to change text"
6. Erase the text on the next screen and enter your quote - click "save and close" when you're done
7. You can scroll through various font, style and color options, move the quote around on the screen by dragging the text box or change the size of the text area by pinching and dragging the text
8. When you're done click "save" in the top right corner - the app will automatically save the image to your camera roll.

# Wrap Up

So that's it! I feel like I should hand you a diploma with a beautiful gold seal and tell you "well done!" **Head to bit.ly/cbcertificate - I created for you in Canva ;)**

Because even if you don't love everything you created, or you're still not sure about some of the steps, making it the whole way through this course is no small thing.

If I can be honest with you, there are A LOT of images on my site that I'd love to change, simply because every time I learn a new skill or find a new tool, I realize how much better my images COULD be.

But as long as we keep trying, keep growing, and keep learning, we're well on our way! My job puts me in a position to create several social media images every day, and my blog requires the same work. It takes practice, it takes being willing to start over when it's going the way you planned, and it takes courage.

- Make the image.
- Add it to your blog post.
- Share it to Instagram.
- Update your Facebook page.
- Create the printable.

Take a deep breath and click "publish." You'll never regret the art you create, but you might regret not making it.


*Many thanks to Katrina Lee, Heidi Guyer, and Janelle Allen for always encouraging and supporting me. Thank you to my husband Matt who cheers for me even when he doesn't understand what I'm talking about {wink}. And last, but not least, to the amazing #creativebasics community – there is good in the world, and on the internet, and you are it, friends.*

*With love,*

*Crystal*

# About the Author

A self-proclaimed "digital missionary" Crystal has always dreamed of her perfect career, climbing the corporate ladder, and achieving success. And she did – and then God began redefining hustle, taking Crystal on a journey from striving to serving. From corporate America to non-profits and freelance work, Crystal understands the tempting pull of striving but has learned to lean into the blessing of focusing her "holy hustle" toward serving God's kingdom.

Mama to a 5-year-old (and married to her high school sweetheart), Crystal is the author of "Creative Basics: 30 Days to Awesome Social Media Art," creator of the popular "Clarity Coaching" Course, editor of "Craving Connection" and host of the annual Write 31 Days challenge, Crystal writes regularly at **crystalstine.me** and can be found on Instagram @crystalstine.

Crystal has been featured in LifeWay's "HomeLife" magazine and has spoken at The Declare Conference, Raising Generations Today Conference, Allume, and at several local events. A full list of magazines, podcasts, and blogs where Crystal's work has been featured can be found on her website.